Traveling Light

Traveling Light

POEMS

LINDA PASTAN

W. W. NORTON & COMPANY

New York   London

For information about permission to reproduce selections from this book,
write to Permissions, W. W. Norton & Company, Inc.,
500 Fifth Avenue, New York, NY 10110

For information about special discounts for bulk purchases,
please contact W. W. Norton Special Sales at
specialsales@wwnorton.com or 800-233-4830

Manufacturing by Courier Westford
Book design by JAM Design
Production manager: Anna Oler

Library of Congress Cataloging-in-Publication Data

Pastan, Linda, date.
Traveling light : poems / Linda Pastan. — 1st ed.
p. cm.
ISBN 978-0-393-07907-4
I. Title.
PS3566.A775T73 2011
811'.54—dc22
                          2010034786

W. W. Norton & Company, Inc.
500 Fifth Avenue, New York, N.Y. 10110
www.wwnorton.com

W. W. Norton & Company Ltd.
Castle House, 75/76 Wells Street, London W1T 3QT

1 2 3 4 5 6 7 8 9 0

FOR RACHEL

Who helped with so many of these

———————————

Contents

ix

x

Acknowledgments

I would like to thank the following magazines in which many of these poems first appeared:

The Alaska Quarterly Review; *The American Scholar*; *The Atlantic*; *Chrysalis*; *Five Points*; *The Georgia Review*; *The Gettysburg Review*; *The Michigan Quarterly Review*; *Moment*; *New Letters*; *The New Republic*; *New Works*; *The New Yorker*; *Nimrod*; *Oregon Literary Review*; *The Paris Review*; *Ploughshares*; *Poet Lore*; *Prairie Schooner*; *Slate*; *Shenendoah*; *The Southern Poetry Review*; *West Marin Review*; *The Virginia Quarterly Review*

"Insomnia" was included in *The Best American Poetry* 2009
"The Flood, 2005" was in the anthology *Hurricane Blues*
"Pears" first appeared in *Setting the Table* (Dryad Press)

I would also like to thank Jill Bialosky who has been such a thoughtful editor and Jean Naggar, my agent, who has been with me almost from the start.

I

Years After the Garden

The Burglary

They stole my mother's silver,
melting it down, perhaps,

into pure mineral, worth
only its own weight.

We must eat with our hands now,
grab for food

in this new place of greed,
our table set

only with memories, tarnishing
even as we speak:

my mother holding a shining ladle
in her hand,

serving the broth
to children who will forget

to polish her silver, forget even
to lock the house.

While forks and spoons are divided
from all purpose,

patterns are lost like friezes
after centuries of rain,

and every knife is robbed
of its cutting edge.

Bread

after Lyubomir Levchev

"It seems to be the five stages
of yeast, not grief,
you like to write about,"
my son says,
meaning that bread
is always rising
and falling, being broken
and eaten, in my poems.
And though he is only half serious,
I want to say to him

"bread rising in the bowl
is like breath rising in the body";
or "if you knead the dough
with perfect tenderness,
it's like gently kneading flesh
when you make love."
Baguette . . . pita . . . pane . . .
challah . . . naan: bread is
the universal language, translatable
on the famished tongue.

Now it is time to open
the package of yeast
and moisten it with water,
watching for its fizz,
its blind energy—proofing
it's called, the animate proof
of life. Everything
is ready: salt, flour, oil.
Breadcrumbs are what lead   *manna*
the children home.

Lettuce Heart with Flower Petals

recipe of Marc Meneau, Vézelay, France

There are flowers
on my salad—nasturtiums
with their shield-shaped leaves,

peppery carnations
(from buttonhole
to mouth) and tender violets—

a sprinkling of edible spring
which may take root
deep inside my body.

Will their tendrils wind
around my windpipe, send
their perfume up

and out of my mouth
in flowery words,
even music?

I eat these tiny squab,
these langoustines
so easily,

but I feel like a cannibal
as I chew on rose petals, color
of the heart's bright blood.

Thanksgiving Ghost

Like a palimpsest
with traces of the past
showing through,

our table
recapitulates
her favorite feast:

the iconic bird
with its secret
wishbone;

baskets of Indian corn;
a still life of winter
vegetables;

and there,
three generations down,
her pale blue eyes

watching
from the child's
oblivious face.

Even candles leave behind
invisible fragrance,
and every book

on every shelf
has its half-imagined
sequel.

Anatomy

In the tenement
of the body
generations have left
their mark.

On the stairwell
of bones and the
walls of flesh
illegible words

are scrawled
in invisible ink.
Windows look down
on concrete gardens

where live buds
force themselves
from sticks
of trees.

The genes are doing
their scheduled work.
Clutch the bannister,
hold on tight.

March

A cardinal is back in the tangled branches
of the maple. Edna always said "Red bird,
cold weather," but it's March now,
the buds already pinking on the camellias.
Edna used to roll biscuits before she cleaned our house,
singing "Amazing Grace" as she worked.
When I sent the tape of a poem to a magazine,
her song by chance on the flip side,
they rejected the poem but asked
if they could use "Amazing Grace."
She died last year, and now I think
her serenity was the flip side
of sadness—the grandson
in trouble with the law; the daughter
far away; so many rooms to clean.

My father's birthday punctuates March.
He would be a hundred and ten, and now
I'm three years older than he was when he died,
so many things unspoken between us.
This is the month for remembering, the light
so new it illuminates what we hardly knew we saw:
Edna in the room downstairs, alone;
my father wanting something from me
I didn't know to give.
It's such a mixed-up month, one foot
in winter the other in spring, doing a windy
two-step from past to future;
while outside the cardinal on the leafless tree
performing its own Amazing Grace
is either scolding or serenading us.

On Seeing an Old Photograph

Why are the young so beautiful—
a foal or a fledgling sparrow, head
half hidden in a ruff of feathers;
a human infant with that milky,
demanding innocence;
even an adolescent boy, awkwardness
shadowed by grace, in his own
invisible force field of desire?

Is it to fool us into sacrifice (remember
Stella Dallas, or a parent bird scouring
the ground for grubs)? To lure the unsuspecting
into the old chain-dance of the genes?
I've looked at you on your way to old age
and found you the perfect portrait
of a man—that wave of white hair
and your noble blade of a nose

like some carved artifact
in a museum. But just now
when I saw the photograph
of you at 20, your feet flung
casually up on your desk, a cigarette—
that ivory amulet, dangling
from supple fingers, and the window
behind you filled to the brim

with leafy spring, I was blindsided
by beauty. I wanted to reach out
and stroke your freshly shaved skin,
to return your sly ambiguous smile,
gateway to some seductive secret.
But out of the frame of the picture,
somewhere beyond that very window,
I was still waiting to be born.

Lilacs

I am following lilacs
cluster by
purple cluster

from Whitman's
dooryards in April
north to New York

where my mother's garden
drowns in their scent
even without her.

I remember her gathering them
by the armful, blossoms
as plump and pale

as lavender pillows,
the white ones
paler still, shedding

their tiny florets
like baby teeth
over her polished floors.

Now in late May,
somewhere near Boston
they are still blooming,

their leaves as heart-shaped
as memory itself.
If I keep traveling north

I may finally find myself
somewhere beyond the treeline,
beyond loss.

For though I don't believe
in ghosts, I am haunted
by lilacs.

Pastoral

Every garden dreams
of being Eden: rosebushes
or wildflowers, it hardly matters
as long as the hum of bees
remains peaceable and the door
to the grave stays hidden
beneath a swath of grass.
In the cooling afternoon
each flower relaxes
on its pedestal of stem,
and the gardener too dreams,
under a tree weighted
each fall with apples.

Pears

Some say
it was a pear
Eve ate.
Why else the shape
of the womb,
or of the cello
whose single song is grief
for the parent tree?
Why else the fruit itself
tawny and sweet
which your lover
over breakfast
lets go your pear-
shaped breast
to reach for?

In Eve's Life
after Amichai

In Eve's life
children arrived uninvited
and after a short time
they left again.
Adam went into the fields
and had his laborers for company.
God had his disciples.

In Eve's life
she mourned the freedoms of the garden.
Later, she mourned the children.

The Serpent to Eve

Consider the vanity
of the seasons,

how an April day preens
in a wash of sun;

how the perfumed luxuries
of summer display themselves

with no thought of privations
on the other side of the world;

how November hides the ravages
of time in a cowl of smoke.

Think of how winter ignores
all rules, all boundaries, how its one

vocation is the blinding
dazzlement of snow.

Now gaze at that loveliness
in the mirror. Clothe it

in the weedy greens of summer,
the hammered gold of early fall.

Even the sky stares
at its own blue reflection

in the polished surface
of every lake.

Eve on Her Deathbed

In the end we are no more than our own stories:
mine a few brief passages in the Book,
no further trace of plot or dialogue.
But I once had a lover no one noticed
as he slipped through the pages, through
the lists of those begotten and begetting.
Does he remember our faltering younger selves,
the pleasures we took while Adam,
a good bureaucrat, busied himself
with naming things, even after Eden?
What scraps will our children remember of us
to whom our story is simple
and they themselves the heroes of it?

I woke that first day with Adam for company,
and the tangled path I would soon follow
I've tried to forget: the animals, stunned
at first in the forest; the terrible, beating wings
of the angel; the livid curse of childbirth to come.
And then the children themselves,
loving at times, at times unmerciful.
Because of me there is just one narrative
for everyone, one indelible line from birth to death,
with pain or lust, with even love or murder
only brief diversions, subplots.

But what I think of now,
in the final bitterness of age,
is the way the garden groomed itself
in the succulent air of summer—each flower
the essence of its own color; the way even
the serpent knew it had a part it had to play, if
there were to be a story at all.

Years After the Garden

Years after the garden closed on Adam
a thousand thousand gardens take its place
(hold my hand, I hear the waters rising)
roses, lemons, lilac, hemlock, grape.

A thousand thousand gardens take its place.
Is each an Eden waiting to be lost?
Roses, lemons, lilac, hemlock, grape.
What was God thinking when he made the apple?

Is each an Eden waiting to be lost?
Seeds of knowledge, carelessness, and greed.
What was God thinking when he made the apple?
Did he do it only for the story?

Seeds of knowledge, carelessness, and greed—
they say the ice cap is already melting.
Did he do it only for the story?
Meringues of childhood melted on the tongue.

They say the ice cap is already melting.
The angel still waits with his flaming sword.
Meringues of childhood melted on the tongue,
but innocence alone will never save us.

The angel still waits with his flaming sword:
flowers and vegetables, forests tremble.
Innocence alone will never save us.
How beautiful the world is in the morning.

Flowers and vegetables, forests tremble.
How beautiful the world is in the morning.
Years ago the garden closed on Adam.
Hold my hand, I hear the waters rising.

2

Time and the Weather

The Maypole
after Wallace Stevens

One must have a mind of spring
to regard the cherry tree burdened
with blossom;

and have been warm for days
to behold the boughs of the redbud
prickly with color in the glint

of the April sun; and not to think
of any cruelty in the difficult birthing
of so many leaves, to feel only pure

elation at the sound of the undulant breeze
which is the sound of every garden
with a breeze blowing among its flowers,

the sound the listener hears, watching the buds
which were not quite here a week ago
pushing up from oblivion now.

Tulips

Robed in purple,
the tulips are open
so wide

they could be a chorus
exulting
in the high notes,

uvulas spilling gold
on my white
tablecloth.

Purple

A bruised evening sky hurts more
than absolute darkness:

purple should be the color
of mourning.

These purple crocuses
erupt from earth

in the exact spot
(under the crooked dogwood)

where last year's blossoms
were stripped

of every waxy petal.
Do flowers mourn?

Is the vernal equinox
a celebration, or a gathering

of the innocent to a place
of eventual frost?

April comforts
and mocks

these brittle bones,
this unwieldy heart

which at the first chime
of spring, rises

(despite itself)
on its purpling stem.

April

A whole new freshman class
of leaves has arrived

on the dark twisted branches
we call our woods, turning

green now—color of
anticipation. In my 76th year,

I know what time and weather
will do to every leaf.

But the camellia swells
to ivory at the window,

and the bleeding heart bleeds
only beauty.

Cows

You're always mentioning cows,
how they're sorrowful, or stodgy,
or simply ruminative; how just
because you like milk is not a reason
to meet one, though I wouldn't mind,
particularly on a nice day in a meadow;
and I'd like to meet that author too
whose books I liked, though he is
the one you're really talking about,
not cows at all. When I was 12
I tried to milk a cow, but though
I tugged and tugged no milk
would come: that cow had teats
like rows of rubber gloves, big eyes,
a wicked tail, and I thought of her
when I nursed my first child.
Now here we are in the car driving west
past painted barns and horses
and yes past cows, and our children
have grown beyond milk, and I often
feel like a cow myself, part stodgy,
part sorrowful, and much too ruminative.

Late September Song

With the sound of
a freight train
rushing
through the trees,
the first strong
wind

of autumn
makes each
leaf
sing the song
of its own
execution.

Bronze Bells of Autumn

Although I've made a kind of peace
with those I loved who are already dead,
bronze bells of autumn, in their minor key,
toll for the losses still ahead.

The weather tells a narrative of change;
the wind prepares a path the geese will take.
This frost is beautiful, and yet it kills.
The harvest moon drowns in the lake.

I love the dark (it moves so gradually)
but love still more all it will erase:
these swarming leaves, this pungent smoky air,
the youth you were, your aging face.

Acorns

a rat-tat-tat
like gunfire
on the tin roof
acorns
are falling
all from a single
tree, a barrage
of acorns
covers the grass
with shells, acorns
as hard as the
casings of bullets
their noisy artillery
keeping us up
at night
so many acorns
all from one tree
relentless
as rookies:
their thwack
after thwack at
batting practice
where are the squirrels?
the gardeners
with rakes?
the farmgirls
their aprons brimming
with acorns to grind
into meal?
the dog cowers
beside the house
the cat hides
under the car
afraid of

the clattering hooves
of acorns
later big oaks
will grow, a forest
of oak trees their roots
will strangle
this house
listen, listen

Vertical

Perhaps the purpose
of leaves is to conceal
the verticality
of trees
which we notice
in December
as if for the first time:
row after row
of dark forms
yearning upwards.
And since we will be
horizontal ourselves
for so long,
let us now honor
the gods
of the vertical:
stalks of wheat
which to the ant
must seem as high
as these trees do to us,
silos and
telephone poles,
stalagmites
and skyscrapers.
But most of all
these winter oaks,
these soft-fleshed poplars,
this birch
whose bark is like
roughened skin
against which I lean
my chilled head,
not ready
to lie down.

Noel

Like a single
ornament,

the red cardinal
on a pine

outside
the window

is our only
decoration,

until
the snow.

Flowers

The deep strangeness
of flowers in winter—

the orange of clivia,
or this creamy white rose

in its stoneware
vase, while outside

another white
like petals drifting down.

Is it real?
a visitor asks,

meaning the odd magenta
orchid on our sill

unnatural
as makeup on a child.

It's freezing all around us—
salt cold on the lips,

the flinty blacks and grays
of January in any northern city,

and flowers
everywhere:

in the supermarket
by cans of juice,

filling the heated stalls
near the river—

secular lilies engorged
with scent,

notched tulips, crimson
and pink, ablaze

in the icy
corridors of winter.

Tannenbaum

It's almost March, and the Christmas tree
is still sitting on the deck where we put it,
temporarily, the day after New Year's.
But now a bird, in fact a whole family
of birds—wrens I think, have built
a nest among its branches
and go busily in and out all day
like thrifty housewives, using strands
of leftover tinsel to decorate their nest.
How can I, who shouldn't have had
a Christmas tree at all, evict them,
dragging the tree to the far end of the gully
where all the other trees I shouldn't have had
ended up: stripped by the weather
of their needles; mere skeletons of themselves?
For though birds aren't human they are
fellow creatures, particularly wrens
who seem so domestic in a fifties kind of way.
Meanwhile the tree just sits there
next to the sculptures of Adam and Eve,
the wrought iron goat, the ceramic turtle.
And if our deck become a makeshift Eden,
must one of us impersonate the serpent?

3

Clock

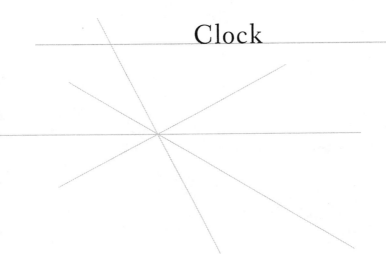

Insomnia

I remember when my body
was a friend,

when sleep like a good dog
came when summoned.

The door to the future
had not started to shut,

and lying on my back
between cold sheets

did not feel
like a rehearsal.

Now what light is left
comes up—a stain in the east,

and sleep, reluctant
as a busy doctor,

gives me a little
of its time.

The Moment

What can I say in this moment
before you leave—
summer leached
of its clear pastels,
the fueled sunlight on your skin
still warm to my mouth,
though fading?

Autumn, that turncoat,
waits at the edge
of the woods with the first
darkening leaves.
And I feel the world move
under our feet on its way
from solstice to solstice.

An involvement in light
presupposes an acquaintance
with shadow, Rothko said.
Didn't he mean us?
Didn't he mean the way
we've waited for this moment
all summer long?

After a Month of Rain

Everything I thought I wanted
is right here,
particularly when the sun
is making such a comeback,

and the lilac engorged
with purple has recovered
from its severe pruning,
and you will be back soon

to dispel whatever it is
that overtakes me like leaf blight,
even on a day like this. I can still
hear remnants of the rain

in the swollen stream
behind the house, in the faint
dripping under the eaves,
persistent as memory.

And all the things I didn't think
I wanted, cut like the lilac back
to the root, push up again
from underground.

The moon

has been missing
for nearly a week; and
you haven't called.

There may be
no connection,
but darkness

is contagious
and blood brother
to silence.

A Dozen Roses

Their stems in the glass vase
are the color
of beet greens,

and their tight purplish blooms
the size and shape
of summer beets.

If only you had brought me
beets instead of
these formal flowers.

If only you had dressed them
in oil and lemon,
caressed them

with sour cream,
we could feast until
our mouths were as red

as the beets themselves,
then bruise those mouths
saltily against each other.

Clock

Sometimes it really upsets me—
the way the clock's hands keep moving,

even when I'm just sitting here
not doing anything at all,

not even thinking about anything
except, right now, about that clock

and how it can't keep its hands still.
Even in the dark I picture it, and all

its brother and sister clocks and watches,
even sundials, all those compulsive timepieces

whose only purpose seems to be
to hurry me out of this world.

Return to Maple 9

Here I am, back
in my own past, river
and meadows exquisitely
the same, only my face
disguised by fifteen years.

In this closet
the very hangers I left—
question marks over the pole—
soon will be clothed
in the livery of age.

The past is the underside
of the future. Remember
the yellow sundress? Remember
the heat of the motorcycle
raging down the road?

Why doesn't the landscape
seem to age? Outside
the old mountain waits
us out, still mute,
still greening.

Counting Backwards

How did I get so old,
I wonder,
contemplating
my 67th birthday.
Dyslexia smiles:
I'm 76 in fact.

There are places
where at 60 they start
counting backwards;
in Japan
they start again
from one.

But the numbers
hardly matter.
It's the physics
of acceleration I mind,
the way time speeds up
as if it hasn't guessed

the destination—
where look!
I see my mother
and father bearing a cake,
waiting for me
at the starting line.

Any Woman

I am neither the crinkled face
in the mirror nor the one
in the photograph, young
and frowning.
Sometimes I am the sleeper
who wakes and like Eve
thinks it is the first morning,
dew on all the silken surfaces
of the world.

Age has nothing to do with me.
Lust still raises its purple flag
and envy its green one—
don't I repent the same sins
every year, make the same resolutions?
When I was a child I had an old face,
and my mother who comforted me then
comforts me still
in her invisible arms.

Alone, I am any woman
fresh from the shower,
covering the newly rained upon
continent of her body—hills and valleys—
modestly with a towel.
Later, someone on the bus stands up
and offers his seat.
Who can it be for? I am
the only one standing.

Thesis

They gave me the unfinished novels
of Hawthorne to study—
signposts, each one,
to all that may lie ahead
for a young writer; object lessons
on the failures of old age.

Image and metaphor were leached
of their earlier powers—
scarlet fading to pink,
sentences going utterly astray.
Dr. Grimshaw and Septimus Felton,
spider and shadow haunted

the old man's dreams.
They placed those manuscripts
on his coffin to follow him
even into the afterlife,
the first clods of earth
darkening the page.

I was 20, cocky, judgmental.
How could I know then
the double-edged sword
language can be to the writer,
what wounds it can inflict, if only
you wield it long enough.

Q and A

I thought I couldn't be surprised:
"Do you write on a computer?" someone
asks, and "Who are your favorite poets?"
and "How much do you revise?"

But when the very young woman
in the fourth row lifted her hand
and without irony inquired:
"Did you write

your Emily Dickinson poem
because you like her work,
or did you know her personally?"
I entered another territory.

"Do I really look that old?"
I wanted to reply, or "Don't
they teach you anything?"
or "What did you just say?"

The laughter that engulfed
the room was partly nervous,
partly simple hilarity.
I won't forget

that little school, tucked
in a lovely pocket of the South,
or that girl whose face
was slowly reddening.

Surprise, like love, can catch
our better selves unawares.
"I've visited her house," I said.
"I may have met her in my dreams."

Ash

We fall like leaves,
anonymous as snow,
like ash, like weeds
under some farmer's hoe.

We fear the dark
and watch the light recede.
We know death smiles
on every child conceived.

The moon goes on
relentless in the sky;
in cold complicity
the stars comply.

Remember me.
(How did it grow so late?)
Anonymous,
I turn the page. I wait.

4

Somewhere in the World

Silence

"The language of war is victims."
—KHALID SHAIKH MOHAMMED, terrorist, *New York Times*

If the language of war
is victims,
choose silence.

If its verbs are bullets
seeking their place
in a sentence,

choose silence.
Over the ruined markets
and smoldering streets

the grammar of pain
has exploded
on every tongue;

not even the vowels
of grief are left
to tarnish the air.

The angel of silence
has flown overhead.
Death too is silent.

In the Forest

The trees are lit
from within like Sabbath candles
before they are snuffed out.
Autumn is such a Jewish season,
the whole minor key of it.
Hear how the wind trembles
through the branches, vibrato
as notes of cello music.
Notice the tarnished coppers
and browns, the piles of leaves
just waiting for burning.
Though birds are no longer
in hiding, though children in bright
scarves are kicking the leaves,
I smell the smoke
and remember winter.
Praise what is left.

Times Square, 1944

The sailors wore their caps
at a cocky angle, like white seabirds
about to take flight;

they moved in a roiling surf
through the traffic,
looking at women

in spiky heels
and hats,
not looking at me.

I was almost thirteen.
The city erupted around me:
kaleidoscope

of noise and lights;
and those sailors
on their hard way somewhere—

I longed to reach
out, I longed to reach out
and embrace them.

Somewhere in the World

Somewhere in the world
something is happening
which will make its slow way here.

A cold front will come to destroy
the camellias, or perhaps it will be
a heat wave to scorch them.

A virus will move without passport
or papers to find me as I shake
a hand or kiss a cheek.

Somewhere a small quarrel
has begun, a few overheated words
ignite a conflagration,

and the smell of smoke
is on its way;
the smell of war.

Wherever I go I knock on wood—
on tabletops or tree trunks.
I rinse my hands over and over again;

I scan the newspapers
and invent alarm codes which are not
my husband's birthdate or my own.

But somewhere something is happening
against which there is no planning, only
those two aging conspirators, Hope and Luck.

Weights and Measures

"a promise weighs more than a country . . ."
—HA JIN

If a promise weighs more
than a country, does love
weigh more than a promise?
Wouldn't I break my word,
wrap myself in any flag (stars,
or sickle, or rising sun) just
to be with you? And how much

does a country weigh?
Its mountains may be heavy—
snow in winter, the dark
cuneiform shapes of pinecones
in summer, but its streams
run lightly through all the fields
of our discarded childhoods.

Sometimes I think a promise
weighs nothing at all, though
it can tether you like an invisible
kite string. And love?
When you leave, it is its absence
that is heavy, as heavy as those
snow-encumbered mountains.

Boundaries

In Monet's *Water Lilies*,
willows dissolve into
flowers dissolve into water,
and form becomes a dream
in purples and blues
without scent or story.
Consider the death of boundaries,
the way sight dissolves
the moment just before sleep
overtakes us. The way
a man can disappear
inside a woman. I remember
a day of ruffling waters
when we sailed west
in your creaky boat.
We steered for the horizon—
that penciled-in line between
ocean and sky, then watched
as it receded ahead of us.
The night my mother died
there were cells in her body
that didn't notice. For a while
the moons of her nails kept rising,
the hair kept growing from the apex
of her widow's peak.
Now by a barbed wire fence
that divides two countries,
the invisible roots of an old tree
spread their living network
underground, in all directions.

Three Skulls on an Oriental Rug
Cézanne, oil on canvas

Whose skulls are these,
and isn't it dread
that informs our pleasure

in this canvas?
A still life, we're told,
is simply the marriage

of form and color to create
a design—a razzle-dazzle circuit
between eye and heart.

So if the objects
are skulls it shouldn't matter,
although we each carry

our own skeleton with us,
skull and all,
up the marble staircase

and into this gallery.
To leach the personal
from the abstract

is a different kind of death.
What we see is more
than a brilliant oriental shape

bleeding its dense
flowery purples and reds   Beauty
under three ovoid objects.   Death

Turner, Late Painting

This almost empty
canvas
is sister
to an empty page
just as a poem
enters: white

with all
its possibilities
emerging
from the brush—
smoke or cloud
or beach foam—

and there in the corner
a patch
of burnt orange
where the sun will
eventually
come up.

On the Steps of the Jefferson Memorial

We invent our gods
the way the Greeks did,
in our own image—but magnified.
Athena, the very mother of wisdom,
squabbled with Poseidon
like any human sibling
until their furious tempers
made the sea writhe.

Zeus wore a crown
of lightning bolts one minute,
a cloak of feathers the next,
as driven by earthy lust
he prepared to swoop
down on Leda.
Despite their power,
frailty ran through them

like the darker veins
in the marble of these temples
we call monuments.
Looking at Jefferson now,
I think of the language
he left for us to live by.
I think of the slave
in the kitchen downstairs.

Anniversary

For us it was the anniversary
of love—September 11th,
the day my parents met, a year later
the day they married.
So when I see or hear that date,

my heart by habit lifts
for a moment, just before
it plunges—history's
dirty thumbprint
staining the calendar.

The Flood, 2005

When Noah prepared his ark
he had precise instructions from above:
so many ribs of cypress covered with reeds,
so many portholes and doors
and where to place them. He was told
how to choose the animals—the pair
of ostriches trying to hide their heads,
the hummingbirds hovering
over the cardinals' red wings,
pigs and camels—all the species
already invented or continuing to evolve.

The rain started slowly: a mist,
a drizzle—drumbeats in the distance becoming
a roar, a world, a very universe of water,
and in those stormy howls Noah discerned
the cadence of punishment.
At the end, God's temper blew itself out
in a final furious burst of wind.
The dove was sent to find dry land,
the sun returned as if it had simply
taken some casual detour, and God went
about his usual business, *ignoring appeals*

somewhere else.
Who worried about the children
still stranded on their failing rooftops;
the abandoned animals
who didn't make it to the ark;
the way so many deaths seemed
an almost incidental part of the story?
Did anyone give instructions
from above, and when?
And if there was sin involved,
wasn't it miles north of the Delta? *D.C.*

Listening to Bob Dylan, 2005

Little Bobby Zimmerman,
did he have a mother?
Iconoclast to icon,
was the wind his brother?

Did he steal or borrow
Woody's voice, pure gravel?
Women gave their bodies.
Kerouac gave travel.

Some would call him genius
or curly-headed sphinx,
riding music out of sight
and noisy as a lynx.

Here we go again,
counting up our dead:
syncopated bullets,
hard rain on our heads,

foxes in the hen house,
freedom on the rack.
Somebody sing something!
The times are a-changin' back.

5

Traveling Light

Flight

They have examined
our luggage, made me
remove my shoes
and then my scarf, as if
I might strangle someone
in its silky purple.
But they let my fear
of flight on board,
though its weight
and turbulence might
bring down any plane.
I signed on for this,
I tell myself, as I did
that other June so long ago,
walking down another aisle
with you, and only
a vague idea of love
to keep us aloft.

X
Time Travel

Elizabeth would choose
The Middle Ages
when cathedrals grew
like stalagmites
out of hard ground,
and rainbows coalesced
to stained glass.

David would choose the 17th century.
He'd whisper in the ear
of Galileo about dark matter
and space explorers; he'd tell him
never mind The Church,
you're canonized in all the textbooks.

Rachel might pick the 19th century,
a country house like the ones in Jane Austen;
or a dacha perhaps, outside of Moscow,
despite the fierce cold,
not to mention the increasingly
angry peasants.

But I would simply choose May 1932
the moment I was born on the Grand Concourse.
I'd insinuate myself into the head
of that girl baby, living her life
all over again
but doing it right this time.   karma

In an Unaddressed Envelope

Dear lovers I never met,
dear children I never carried,
you who were here for a while
clothed in the rags of imagination,
who brushed past me without seeing
and sang songs the wind carried away
as if they were so many leaves
to be raked and burned later:
your singing comes back to me now
beneath the dark elusive notes
of someone else's music.

There are so many faces in the world,
so many seeming strangers, and yet
I see your smoky hair, your eyes
through the window of a train that rushes past
with the swooshing sound of distances.
Listen. I know you wait for me
at a place I am always seeking.
You are as real as the changelings
in my favorite books, have the tenderness
of the sea on a calm day, and all
the patience of the long invisible.

photos,jacket

Three Perfect Days

In the middle seat of an airplane,
between an overweight woman
whose arm takes over the armrest
and a man immersed in his computer game,

I am reading the inflight magazine
about three perfect days somewhere: Kyoto
this time, but it could be anywhere—
Madagascar or one of the Virgin Islands.

There is always the perfect hotel
where at breakfast the waiter smiles
as he serves an egg as perfectly coddled
as a Spanish Infanta.

There are walks over perfect bridges—their spans
defying physics—and visits to zoos
where rain is forbidden,
and no small child is ever bored or crying.

I would settle now for just one perfect day
anywhere at all, a day without
mosquitoes, or traffic, or newspapers
with their headlines.

A day without any kind of turbulence—
certainly not this kind, as the pilot tells us
to fasten our seatbelts, and even
the flight attendants look nervous.

In the Har-Poen Tea Garden

Three, nine, seventeen
carp—one for each syllable
color the water.

A sip of green tea—
the very taste of Japan,
odd but comforting.

The old maple bows
with such strict formality
over the fish pond.

I long for free verse,
explosions of syllables,
but this is Japan.

In white wedding dress
a bride bows down the stone path,
West and East marry.

Poor blooming cherry
trapped in miniature beauty.
The spell is bonsai.

Freed from a painting,
a ceremonial crane
fishes for dinner.

I dream in haiku—
words as perfect as blossoms
gone in the morning.

Driving West

Though the landscape subtly changes,
the mountains are marching in place.

The grasses take on the fading
yellows of the sun,

and cows with their sumptuous eyes
litter the fields as if they had grown there.

We have driven for hours
through bluing shadows,

as if the continent itself leaned west
and we had no choice but to follow the old ruts—

the wagons and horses, the iron snort
of a locomotive. We are the pioneers

of our own histories, drawn
to the horizon as if it waited just for us

the way the young are drawn
to the future, the old to the past.

L·H Moon

String Lake, Wyoming

Below the
staggered peaks
of the Tetons,
swathed today
in cloud,
this green
shallow lake
is on its way
to becoming
a meadow—
flowers waiting
somewhere
in the future,
yellow and blue,
the way words
waited once
along the primeval
shores
of language.

Early

> "Despite her delaying tactics,
> she would still be morbidly punctual."
> —YAEL HEDAYA, *Accidents*

I am never merely punctual,
I am always early. Sometimes I wait
in doctors' offices, on the threshold
of some pending grief. Or I sit
in expectantly empty rooms
while upstairs my hostess casually
screws in an earring. I am early
for trains which haven't yet left

their previous stations. I pace the platform
under a clock which moves its ancient hands
only by stealth. Think of what I could do
with all the squandered minutes I spend
just standing around rereading the face
of my watch, as if it had more than time to tell.
On nights when you arrive precisely
on time, and I have been waiting

precisely twenty minutes, I can't help
being angry. "Morbidly punctual?"
she must have meant morbidly early,
meant someone like me, afraid
of being late and missing my life.
But I am already practicing
for my death, wondering how long
it will keep me waiting.

Recycled

"This Book Of Poems Has Been Printed On Recycled Paper"

Isn't it a form of reincarnation—
the sports page or an ad for vitamins
becoming, miraculously, the space
where a love poem finds itself?

a discarded shopping list
(cereal, oranges, soap)
returning to life as the backdrop
for a sonnet or villanelle?

I stare at each recycled page
and think about pentimento:
could lines from a diary
or a discarded prayer book

work their way through
these measured stanzas, lending
mysterious rhythms and weight
to another generation of words?

As when we put a loved body
in the ground, expecting finality,   *palimpsest*
and the newly nourished grass
exuberantly grows over it.

At the Riverside Chapel

When they gave her son
her wedding ring
he knew she was really dead
and being stripped down
for that final
passage—

bare hands crossed;
naked under
a simple dress;
the kind of frugality
she would have
disdained,

preferring those
sumptuous robes,
those jewels
the pharaohs wore
when they pushed off
on the same journey.

The Ordinary

It may happen on a day
of ordinary weather—
the usual assembled flowers,
or fallen leaves
disheveling the grass.
You may be feeding the dog,
or sipping a cup of tea,
and then: the telegram;
or the phone call;
or the sharp pain traveling
the length of your
left arm, or his.
And as your life is switched
to a different track
(the landscape
through grimy windows
almost the same though
entirely different) you wonder
why the wind doesn't
rage and blow as it does
so convincingly
in Lear, for instance.
It is pathetic fallacy
you long for—the roses
nothing but their thorns,
the downed leaves
subjects for a body count.
And as you lie in bed
like an effigy of yourself,
it is the ordinary
that comes to save you—
the china teacup waiting
to be washed, the old dog
whining to go out.

The Still Point

In the suspension
for a moment
of breath,

in the rattle
of a woodpecker piercing
the very heart,

the sun fixes
each shadow
in its place,

the wind moving
from past to future blows
itself out,

and I lie still
in the simple perfection
of the present.

Even so, the worm
of language
penetrates,

for the mind itself
refuses
to shut down

though heat
and blossoms
and body

merge,
if only
for a moment.

Traveling Light

I'm only leaving you
for a handful of days,
but it feels as though
I'll be gone forever—
the way the door closes

behind me with such solidity,
the way my suitcase
carries everything
I'd need for an eternity
of traveling light.

I've left my hotel number
on your desk, instructions
about the dog
and heating dinner. But
like the weather front

they warn is on its way
with its switchblades
of wind and ice,
our lives have minds
of their own.